IN VISIBLE INK

Selected Shorter Poems, 1955-1979

ROBERTO SANESI

Translated from Italian by

William Alexander, T.G. Bergin, Richard Burns, Cid Corman,
Giuliano Dego, Martin Dodman, Michael Edwards, T.H. Jones,
Margaret Straus, Vernon Watkins and Clive Wilmer

PROSPICE 13

Guest Edited by Richard Burns

AQUILA

PROSPICE

Edited by J.C.R. Green and Michael Edwards.
Published by Aquila Publishing Company,
a trading division of
JOHNSTON GREEN & Co. (PUBLISHERS) LTD.
P.O. Box 1, Portree, Isle of Skye, Scotland IV51 9BT

Manuscripts for consideration should be sent to either J.C.R. Green at the publishers, or Michael Edwards, 30 Alma Street, Wivenhoe, Essex CO7 9DL. Return postage in British stamps or international reply coupons must be enclosed. While every care is taken of submissions, no responsibility can be accepted for loss or damage, however caused.

British Library Cataloguing in Publication Data

Sanesi, Roberto
  In visible ink — (Prospice ISSN 0308-2776; v.13)
  I. Title   II. Burns, Richard 19----
  III. Series
  851' .914   PQ4841.S/

ISBN 0 7275 0255 7

ACKNOWLEDGEMENTS

Many of these translations have been published in the following collections, anthologies or periodicals: *Angels Disturb Me*, by Roberto Sanesi, tr. William Alexander; *Directions in Italian Poetry*, ed. Giuliano Dego and Margaret Straus; *Granta*, tr. Richard Burns; *Grosseteste Review*, tr. Cid Corman; *Harvard Bulletin*, tr. William Alexander; *Homage to Mandelstam*, ed. Richard Burns and George Gömöri; *Italian Sampler*, tr. T.H. Bergin; *Journey Toward the North*, by Roberto Sanesi, tr. William Alexander; *Learning to Talk*, by Richard Burns; *The Literary Review*, tr. Clive Wilmer; *London Magazine*, tr. Giuliano Dego and Margaret Straus; *Mediterranean Review*, tr. William Alexander; *Michigan Quarterly Review*, tr. William Alexander; *The New Republic*, tr. William Alexander; *Origin*, tr. Cid Corman; *Ploughshares*, tr. William Alexander; *PN Review*, tr. Michael Edwards; *Poetry Wales*, tr. Richard Burns; *Roberto Sanesi: A Selection*, ed. Tim Longville, tr. William Alexander, Cid Corman and Vernon Watkins; *Selected Verse Translations* by Vernon Watkins; and *Songs of a Mad Prince* by T.H. Jones.

I should also like to thank Roberto Sanesi for his constant help, advice and encouragement through all the stages of preparing this book for publication; Michael Edwards, for his patient and constructive criticism and advice, with both individual texts and the book as a whole; the other translators of the poems, with several of whom I have engaged in lengthy discussion and correspondence; the Arts Council of Great Britain, for the fellowship in creative writing (at the Victoria Centre for Adult Education, Gravesend, Kent, 1979-81), which afforded me time to work on this edition; and Joan Hall, Rachel Patterson, Paola Pinna, Frances Richards and Gwen Watkins. Two of the writers whose translations are included in this anthology, T.H. Jones and Vernon Watkins, will never have the chance to read it, and nor will Ceri Richards, whose illustrations for *Journey Toward the North* were among the last works he composed before his death. This book is a testament to their memory.

R.B., Cambridge and Gravesend, January 1981

CONTENTS

INTRODUCTION

I

Roberto Sanesi was born in 1930 in Milan, where he still lives. His first full-length collection of poetry came out twenty-four years ago. Since then, hardly a year has gone by without his publishing at least one book, whether of poems, criticism, drama or translation. His writing is as consistent as it is prolific, and its deepest roots are in a thoroughly native tradition stretching back through the masters of the *Duecento* to the Latin poets. Sanesi has special regard for Cavalcanti, for the Dante of the *Rime* as well as of the *Commedia*, and for Lucretius among the Latins — all poets who celebrate '*il ben del intelletto*'. Apart from this, and many textural features in his work, the depth of his Italian sensibility is nowhere more clearly seen than in his constant questioning of aesthetic and philosophical theories in the act of making the poem itself, and in his passionate involvement with the visual arts and music as well as poetry. Much of his finest criticism has been on painting and sculpture.

When it comes to more recent influence, however, Sanesi is far from being typically Italian. For many years he has been regarded in Italy as a 'difficult' poet, not just for the surface density of his language, but because his work has taken few, if any of its bearings either from the mainstream tradition of twentieth century Italian poetry (Ungaretti, Montale, Quasimodo, Saba, etc.) or from the conventional Italian avant-garde from, say, the futurists to Pasolini. Since his early twenties he has been more attracted to British and American poetry and to French surrealist and structuralist writers than to any recent models in his own country, and the long list of his translations from English in the bibliography at the end of this book shows clearly where his roots and affinities are to be looked for, at least among the moderns. The act of translation, a reading which is also a writing, necessarily involves an integration of the linguistic patterns and cultural assumptions underlying the source-text into the translator's own consciousness at a deep level, all of which in their turn both challenge, modify and invigorate his thought-processes, relationship to his own traditions, customs, etc., and linguistic behaviour in his own writing. In Sanesi's case, the extent of this assimilation from English language texts has been enormous: he has translated, among others, the work of Marlowe, the Metaphysicals, Blake, Shelley, Byron, Poe, Whitman, Yeats, Hart Crane, Conrad Aiken, T.S. Eliot, Dylan Thomas, and Vernon Watkins, and is now working on the first new version of *Paradise Lost* to have appeared in Italian for the last hundred years. Sanesi's work as a translator has undoubtedly given him a breadth and depth of resonance in his own writing, making him unusual and perhaps even unique in this respect among contemporary Italian poets. His obvious familiarity with British and American culture is also helpful in providing the reader with a point of entry to his own poems in English translation; although here, perhaps, it is just as well to emphasise that to regard his strong affinities and sympathies with our own literature as more important than his rootedness in a much older native tradition is to invite a distorted reading.

All the same, many features of Sanesi's work do show a scope perhaps more familiar to readers of twentieth-century English language poetry than to their Italian counterparts: for example, the intellectual and sensory challenge embodied in his lines, combined with the deliberate distancing from conventional discourse by means of fragmentation of expected syntactical patterns, violation of what Chomsky called 'selection restrictions', and mixing together of language registers; the frequent starkness and unexpectedness of his chains of images; his integration of formal rhetorical devices (e.g. from Latin, *Il Dolce Stil Novo*, etc.) into the rhythms of contemporary speech; and, above all, his constant preoccupation with the long poem or poem-sequence and with 'open form', along with his refusal to be beguiled into the mere mellifluousness of traditional prosody or the mystifying dreaminess of neo-hermeticism (both serious temptations for the Italian poet). Furthermore, both his so-called cerebrality and his interest in a wide range of subjects (history, metaphysics, philosophy, linguistics, psychology, anthropology and architecture, as well as painting, sculpture, music, and so on) show that his prime concern is to explore the coherence and connectedness of civilisation itself rather than the prettification or decoration of localised experience. This range of reference, embedded in his poems, is made fully explicit in his criticism: for example, in his pioneering work on the Welsh painter Ceri Richards, whose European stature he recognised and championed long before most British critics. As an aside here, it should also be mentioned that Sanesi is widely travelled: the zones mapped in his poems range from Milan to Mexico, New York to Swansea, Prague to Provence, London to the Lofoten Islands.

In all these respects, Sanesi's work probably takes its bearings from Pound and Eliot more than from any other twentieth-century poets, although the echoic sonority and intensity of personal passion in writers like Hart Crane, Dylan Thomas and Vernon Watkins have sparked off many echoes in his own lines: the finest example perhaps being his moving 'Elegy for Vernon Watkins'. Pound's influence, which is pervasive, is harder to cite by specific examples, but can be recognised in reviewing both the extent of Sanesi's work as a translator and the extent of influence his translations have had on his own work, and also in his constant concern with self-definition, particularly through long, open-structured poems. Pound's complaint in 'Canto CXVI', that 'I cannot make it cohere', and his reply to himself in the same poem, that 'it coheres all right / even if my notes to not cohere. / Many errors, / a little rightness', may fairly be seen as keys to Sanesi's poetic procedure, for the questioning of values necessarily involves self-appraisal and self-questioning. The poet's inner compulsion to try to make it all 'cohere', together with the simultaneous recognition of the impossibility of ever completely succeeding in doing so, goes back at least as far as Browning, who in 1845 wrote to Elizabeth Barrett: 'I have never begun what I know I was born to begin and end: RB, a poem.' Despite his own increasing sense of failure to 'make RS, a poem', through the 'mid-life crisis', and so on (delineated meticulously in poems like 'Poetry does not improve with the years'), Sanesi too reasserts that 'still, in spite of everything / there is the attempt at unity' ('Desert'). And just as Pound wrote, in the draft for 'Canto CXV', 'but the light sings eternal', so Sanesi too sees the paltriness of his own human attempts at coherence and unity redeemed by constantly repeated chance images of light, music and wind as connecting principles (as in 'Letter I'), and of trees, a huge variety of birds, and 'the amazement of snow' as revelation. As for Eliot's influence, this is more obvious, not so much in terms of affinities of belief (Sanesi does not celebrate Christianity), but of texture, in many direct references and echoes: for example, in 'Resolution', 'April' and, most of all, 'Our Lady of King's Road'. Sanesi is just as capable of lyricism or irony as Eliot or Pound, but is no more confined than they are in any single mode. More important, his 'blessed rage for order', like theirs — and like that of both Dante and Lucretius, embraces not merely the minutiae of personal experience, but also theoretical discourse, and is directed towards interpreting, clarifying and criticising history itself, both as the sum of all such minutiae and as an always imperfect totality whose most constant feature is flux.

To point out these influences and affinities is not, of course, to make impertinent claims about Sanesi's stature: such evaluations are always spurious when made on behalf of a living writer, for the simple reason that it is impossible to predict the future direction of an artist; and Sanesi's work is very much a developing entity. However, it is to argue that his writing belongs within a broader cultural mainstream than that of most of his immediate Italian predecessors and contemporaries, and not, as some of them may have thought, in a small Lombardian tributary. Major movements of thought and ideas in literature have never been confined within national or even linguistic boundaries, any more than they have in science. Broadly speaking, Sanesi's is the major western tradition of modernism, which, it may be argued, is the direct heir of the Italian poets he most admires: Eliot is rooted in Dante, Pound in Cavalcanti. To have pursued this tradition in relative isolation in his own country for many years, and to have done so doggedly and with little recognition, is in itself evidence of Sanesi's seriousness; and the 'difficulty' of his poems perhaps reflects the difficulty of that task.

II

Of all the recurrent themes and image-patterns in Sanesi's work, one in particular must be discussed here, since recognition of it, I believe, unlocks most of the surface difficulties of his texts, and opens the way to a deeper reading. This is his perception of the universe itself in linguistic terms, and his repeated use of linguistic metaphors to approach the stuff of reality, both as '*un système où tout se tient*', as Ferdinand de Saussure said of language, and as a mysterious continuum of transformations. For example, in an early poem, 'False Dedication', we find that 'the demiurge bird / could trace his signs of light between the wires of the grass, could / whistling, reduce the time and space of you / and the reason burning on your face'. Here, the bird's flight and song are not merely part of a reality perceived as perfected or separate either from the poem itself or from the 'you', the observer. They enter the poem in a dynamic way, as part of the process of its being written, just as the bird also has its share in 'writing' the total pattern it is part of, by its very act of flying and singing. There is, in fact, *no* observer: the 'you' in the poem is as much a part of the overall *gestalt* as the bird, and, moreover, is both entered and changed by the bird. That the creature is a 'demiurge' implies both consciousness and creativity, and that it 'traces' its 'signs of light' also points to its act having meaning or reference beyond itself. The poem ends with one of Sanesi's characteristic image-chains: 'rhymes and rocks and creatures endured in this kingdom'. By listing these phenomena together, he emphasises that they are all syllables, words, phrases in the 'writing' which is reality itself. Exactly the same device is used in a later poem, 'Open the Door': 'Open the door, the verse, the wood closet, / the maze, the spider's web, / the myrtle, the mouth'. These are all images of entry and exit, pattern and transformation. Linguistic images abound through all his poems: 'the arch of a door' is 'swarming / with signs' ('Letter VI'); 'We listen to / moving slow behind the eyes the signs / of a barren countryside. In the air / meditated phrases flatten out. You've broken / meaning like bread' ('Mind-Easer / Psycho-Tonic'); 'hammering verbs onto time' ('Continuous Practice'); and 'the waning / light that plucks the word / out of a circle of rain' ('Letter I'). Linguistic images often combine with images of light and music which, as has already been noted, are themselves connecting principles. The universe, then, is conceived as a text which, if one could only stop time dead, would be perfectly written, but since one cannot, is constantly in process of being written — as well as being revised, cancelled, corrected, unwritten and rewritten.

The origin of this notion, which is articulated at the start of St. John's Gospel ('In the beginning was the Word'), is at least as old as *Genesis* and perhaps as ancient as human writing itself. That the universe is a language written by the Creator implies pattern, coherence, meaning — even if its texts sometimes appear indecipherable. Conversely, the fact that humans too have the language-faculty means that we possess some of the sparks of that divine creativity, that magical and transformative power which first set everything in motion: hence shamanism, orphism, poetry, mathematics, etc. This notion is a constant theme among the thinkers of the Italian Renaissance, for example Pico della Mirandola and Giordano Bruno, which once again demonstrates Sanesi's indebtedness to his native tradition. However, the same theme is also expressed in the Gnostic traditions of all the major Western religions — Judaism, Christianity and Islam — and nowhere more articulately and succinctly than in the Cabbalah: the creation of the universe, which is both finite and temporal, necessarily involved not an extension of God, but a diminution, since God is by definition both infinite and eternal. Yet the text which the Creator started writing in the very act of the First Creation was deliberately left incomplete. Humanity's task is to finish writing it and, by doing so, to 'spell the name of God': that is, from within the finite and temporal, to restore the infinite and eternal. A daring notion, that humanity should 'complete' God. It is one, however, which has attracted modern writers as diverse as Jung (in *Answer to Job*), Borges (in *Labyrinths*), and Jabès (in *The Book of Questions*). Sanesi, incidentally, is also an admirer of all of these writers.

Although Sanesi is not a cabbalist, his work is thoroughly imbued with this theme — and, it must be added, far more so than with the influence of the contemporary French structuralists and their concern with 'écriture', 'sign' and so on, or with Chomsky and post-Chomskyan linguistics, both of which areas of thinking he is also familiar with. The theme surfaces in his work in a multitude of ways: most of all, perhaps, in his concern with the process of writing itself as a subject needing exploration again and again in poems, as in 'From the Notes of Keats Before Writing the *Ode to the Nightingale*', or in 'Regulae ad Directionem Ingenii'. I think it would be a mistake to read these poems as merely playful or ironic explorations of the psychology of the artist, even if that element clearly comes into them. The creative act of writing a poem, which they explore, is both itself *and* a symbol for all acts of creation, including the first one. Furthermore, his aim here is both to understand and pin down, however provisionally or imperfectly, the ways in which the written poem connects with the world (itself a larger 'written text') which surrounds and receives it; for the poem not only comments upon the world, but also enters it, and by entering it, is entered — subtly changing it, but also being changed by it. All this links at a deep level (alchemically?) with Sanesi's Poundian search for self-definition and questioning of cultural values. Clumsily stated, the question he finds himself forced to pose, in poem after poem, is something like this: 'How can I, a man and a poet, perceive order within the chaos, fallibility and uncertainty that are myself, and from them create order within my writing which reflects the ordered, but incomplete and often indecipherable text which is already written into the making of all things ever made, including my own confusion, but which my own writing also rewrites?'

The posing of this complex question can sometimes lead Sanesi to despondency and pessimism at the overwhelming impossibility of the task. For example, in 'Thesis', we find that 'the fact / that even the eternal father is a poet / is not enough to convince me fully'. In 'Little Mountain Landscape', the tone is stronger still: 'my writing scratched in the snow / by a dog's back paws, / runs through the gorges, artifice, / the deceitful equestrian tricks / of alphabets in the optics of a hawk.' Here, nature's writing and the poet's are identified in the canine tracks in the snow, just as they are in Ted Hughes's poem 'The Thought Fox' and Sorley MacLean's 'Dogs and Wolves'. But for Sanesi, both 'writings' are read as 'deceitful' by the haughty and merciless eye of the predator above. This is as much as to say, 'What is the point of it all?' when there is such a great gulf between his own attempts to 'make it cohere' and the language being written and read all around him, in nature's signs. This theme, incidentally, is comparable to one constantly reiterated by W.S. Graham: 'What is the language using us for?' And, curiously, Graham too uses the image of a dog's tracks in the snow in a very similar way. (See his books *Malcolm Mooney's Land* and *Implements in Their Places*.) Yet in many of Sanesi's poems, the languages of both nature and poetry are not only identified — as they must be, since the latter is part of the former — but what they are 'using us for' becomes clear, simple and radiant: the invisible ink of the universal text, which is written into 'the folds / of appearances' ('Letter VII'), is both deciphered, revealed and translated within the poem, and nowhere more gracefully and convincingly than in the 'Elegy for Vernon Watkins': 'But you saw the gold eyes of birds / immutable in a verb of clear waters / and air a wavering column of meanings / hung between a motionless butterfly / and mystery stilled in its butterfly wings.' Here again, images of birds, light and language are woven into the same fabric, spelling coherence and revelation. Even within randomness, there is order; even chance, coincidence, hazard, are caught into overall harmony; and aleatory flux is itself a strand in the pattern. This perception of the connectedness of all phenomena involves the intellect completely, but also defies it, and so can never be comprehended fully by the intellect alone. The 'Elegy for Vernon Watkins' ends accordingly with a celebration of the 'demiurge' power of the poet which is simultaneously a proper confession of the poet's limitations: 'In your bones you knew abstract conjecture / could never yield a true equation. Wholly / for this, perhaps, you return. You achieved a match / between your partial vision and time's limitations / and now have taken back that vision's meaning / into the deep but dazzling darkness.' The universal text, then, can never be completely written within time, for time itself is the crack in the jar of eternity, and perfection, if ever contained in the now, leaks through it perpetually into the future, constantly inking new configurations, 'ghostlier demarcations, keener sounds'.

III

To English-speaking readers, Roberto Sanesi is probably best known for his long poem *Information Report* (Cape Goliard Press, London, 1970), in William Alexander's translation. His shorter poems first began to find their way into English around 1960, however, and over the last twenty years many of them have appeared in magazines and small editions on both sides of the Atlantic, as well as in Japan, translated by Cid Corman for his magazine *Origin*. In editing this book, my aim has been simple: I have attempted to gather the best and most representative of all the existing English translations of his shorter poems, by various writers, and also to fill in gaps by commissioning versions of untranslated poems from different periods, in order to present a coherent introduction to his development over a quarter of a century. The work of eleven translators is included — both British, American and Italian, nearly all of them practising poets in their own right. Poems are printed in strict chronological order, with date of composition and translator's initials given below each poem. Roberto Sanesi has given me complete editorial freedom of selection from the whole range of his work, and any misrepresentation resulting from emphasis on particular aspects or phases of it at the expense of others must be attributed to me, not to him. In choosing between two or more existing translations of a particular poem, I have tried in all cases to select the version which I believed worked best in English, did fullest justice to the Italian, and fairly represented the translator. On grounds of length, I had to exclude several fine translations, and was particularly sorry not to be able to include Cid Corman's versions of the 'Eight Improvisations' or the 'Hypotheses' series, or William Alexander's version of 'Harrington Gardens Suite'. Longer poems already published in English but in versions not included in this anthology are listed in the bibliography. Since Sanesi's *forte* is the long, discursive poem, it might be argued, with some justification, that a book consisting entirely of his shorter poems in itself presents a distortion of his work. I hope this fault may be corrected by the future publication of a companion volume of 'Selected Longer Poems'. This book also contains notes to some of the poems, which are intended to help the reader gloss specific references, particularly the names of places and people, rather than to be interpretative. Variations and idiosyncracies in spelling adopted by translators have been adhered to. Finally, the title of the book, *In Visible Ink*, although approved by Roberto Sanesi, was chosen by me, with help from Rachel Patterson; and I hope that the reasons for its adoption are already clear from the preceding section of this introduction.

Richard Burns
Cambridge
January 1981

THE RESOLUTION
to Giò Pomodoro

Flower of stone and thorn in a
sea of stone and thorn and between the essence
and the existence falls
not the Shadow now but light —
falls headlong, sun, if you will,
but thorn and stone and not
upon this stone, and wheels and signs
and sunflowers and faces
with little horns with
wild eyes where mind
would not be and action alone
would live, the one and
only action where the sounds
of clear waters blend in chorus and,
flower of stone and thorn, it may
resolve itself
in one light En Clair.

1955   *(CW)*

THE CRAB

It was at the wave's foot the crab was scrabbling
with rusty pincers wet in the sand, the hidden
labyrinths into the salt and August drowsiness of sun,
the quiet floss-sulking of the foams between
the sticks on the beach veined with small red grains.
He came back in a springing toil of movement.
The vault shook down each time the wave woke up,
with thrusts, with seaweeds, cyclones of sand.
Orpheus' wild beast has now transformed himself.
In the free yoke of the water, repetition, future,
he draws himself up; he arches himself
to orient and impel his vertix,
pincers of living rust, to the heart of the iron
horizon; he pierces the lighter element
with anguish, he shapes it, and wakes himself up in the blue.

1955   *(THJ)*

15

ARC OF LIGHT

Trace an arc of light at the window, a white
flight of sparrows, winter, which never fly
from these walls, and a white flower — a still life,
hostile, made in our image. Renounce
the slender flame on the heights, the snowdrop
given of God, but live among things, join
thread by thread the fable and the idea, the air of freedom
created and recreated in one thrust
of your boughs weighed down with snow. Hark
how silence swarms at the shutters, and how pity
moans in the cold. If the goddess Minerva
does not descend in the night, her eyes
grim with intelligence, we shall charge the heart
with gravity, which draws us down to the earth's centre.

1956   *(CW)*

STATUE OF SALT AND WALL OF HYACINTH

In this poisonous intimacy of trees and wind
(hypothesis and procession) that confines thought
should a day of stars reveal and betray the world
and not express the void, a different
substance comes from our speech, a different
fable and memory, and should it happen,
now and for ever, that the earth also
refuses the cold breath of your heart,
then indeed it is for us to say,
you must not, you do not love, it is too late,
harp of the wind and the will, our fate
is to give a new meaning to truth, a new
embrace to your water-limbs
in an intimacy of dry consents and golden
denials against my sky's white background,
an epic vainly refused to needs and gestures,
statue of salt and wall of hyacinth,
born already keeping a vigil, anciently budded,
beyond the eyes of you become a person.

1956   *(THJ)*

16

FALSE DEDICATION

It was your sign to believe in a future: a kingdom in which to distinguish
the prints of bulls and ghosts upon the unfinished green
of the wave on the wave, in the water sombred by fishes
from rivers pursued by the sea, white winding-sheet
over which to project wounding. But it was also
as a response to an adagio
of symbols and syllables, a liquid encounter
of Nothingness with the To-Be: and then the demiurge bird
could trace his signs of light between the wires of the grass, could,
whistling, reduce the time and space of you,
and the reason burning on your face. This was your kingdom. The darting
     impulse.
The idea of a rose or a pebble. And you, nobody, moving from the
     nothingness
of a thing that is casually born from a thing,
you balanced yourself in the ring's eternal centre:
rhymes and rocks and creatures endured in this kingdom.

1958   *(THJ)*

INCITATUS

      Out of a tufa sky the moonlight
nibbles at the shadows lingering on the lips of the gods and summons
the screech owl forth from his cave. The clepsydra is dry, the eye of the
     emperor
smiles from his column. Rome, unstirring, eternally restless,
hearkens to the Mouth of Truth. In the Forum
the Senator whinnies to his own glory.

1958   *(TGB)*

SWANSEA

Dreary shadows and ferns, seagulls, an assault
of sudden lights — and again the silence glides
as far as Mumbles on the dunes, gasping,
    the silence
              that endears the hedges
of the gardens and hills to red-haired
native whores, if love leads them to reveal
the freckles on their breasts where the shadow is a cry.

I from this silence and from windows open
on the tide that submerges shells and sludge
see caps and pipes of nonconformists
who take with the ladies, cursing
and quoting the Bible,
              tiny bits of toast and a cup of tea.

1958   *(WA)*

OPEN DIALOGUE

              We are
two amid blue celandine, and sometime
shadows (but who falls on your face, who
in my thoughts pursues you if you do not run,
a memory?) of repentance, of pain, in this sky
corroded by twilight, a memory,
for how much hasnt been, and now you seek me
with a voice that is not your own, Answer,
not a tablet where the wind nestles
the spider's retreats, unknown envy, our
impossible love, not this, but with gestures of anger
the shadow leans over my figure, and a figure
the shadow touching me with a cold sound. Answer,
isnt this perhaps why your flame kindles
the celandine? And I look at my hand. We are
two amid the silence of the mind and the silent

18

troubled darkness of what's not been, two shadows
hesitant at the garden wall. Answer, dont you hear
the reverberation of geranium, the mole's bite, a cry
of earth stirred in its thoughts, when the blackbird shakes
remembrance and the branch with a tough beak? Why
wont you ever answer? We would have time and world
if you did not exist.

1958   *(CC)*

THE OBJECT

It swells at dawn — in the cry of insects: the aching silence of sounds.
And in his figure flung into space, a body
tactile and of dimensions as yet unknown, man finds grace with the object,
and space closes and opens afresh.
                                        I observe in the garden
a red-haired dog nibbling daisies, a turf, a swing
riding in the leaves, Ishmael running to the sea, and revelation
is no longer in the shivered light, in the deceitful and propitious iris
of tired eyes, but in the darkness the object proceeds from, an absence
of limit and weight.
                              Every figure is like an empty sound, Ishmael,
a red-haired dog running towards the sea with white, silent petals
on its tongue, and the swing immobile in daylight.

1959   *(ME)*

THE SEA COMMENCES WHERE IT COMES TO AN END

Organs are intoning Mass. And the organs, in the organs,
break through the casing of the pipes and the hollow casing
of the skull, accusers fleeing through the ferns;
and further ahead, on the hill, and the shore, sailors
who perished centuries ago heave to the light
their chests swollen with hollow breaths. I walk.

And his steps as they proceed abandon to the clear,
inextricable silver of wrecks, the lucid
form of our thoughts, a willow wand
that flings to the sea in a twofold advent,
bent in two, its two ends trembling,
awaiting the utter consummation of meaning.

They walk. And there are more than two while I limit myself
to taking note of how they make ready, black
judges accusing, offenders and accused: crows
that nod by fits and jerks at the supple indictments
of gowned plumage when seagulls clamour
white on the benches of sand where they array themselves

immobile and erect. I walk. And if they proceed,
step by step we are priests averse from words.
And now the humblest garment is gathered by the sparrows of Hades
at the ford through the pools. The proceedings instituted are waived.
Organs are intoning Mass. And the organs, in the organs,
break through the hollow casing of the requiescat. The sea

commences just where it ends. The sea within the sea.

Gower Peninsula, 1959   *(ME)*

A VISIT TO THE RUINS OF THE ROMAN CITY OF BATH

> . . . *cynelic thing,*
> *huse . . . burg . . .*

When evening kindled the plain, flickering
among the sparse insects motionless in the corn
burnt by the snow, we knew
that the city was finished, its thoroughfares
a threaded hollow, its windows vacant, the flights
of all its haughty stairs fallen to earth,

the easy chairs and the idols, and also
wheels, and papers, and aerial
on television aerial, and bathrooms
where piping water steams on the ancient stones.

Motionless insects crick
on the ferro-concrete,
'a royal object,
a palace,
a regal city.'

Now we
trample the snow, we talk
of ourselves and of God, with words
hard put to part the air, and maybe
we'll come back again, in summer,
touching stones and climbing the hill
with a stitch. But when I
return to that night, all I remember
is a white space, and a wolf's tongue
warming a sparrow's body.

1959   *(ME)*

THE CUT IN THE ROCK

Light buried in the grain of the rock,
and the cut white with faeces and generations of fish
falls like a blunt shadow, a thing of white light
where bracken sway with hard-backed leaves,
noxious herbs, metal and rock in a lone burst of roots
from an overhanging sky. The varying light has no reflections
when you walk with care. Neither gesture nor voice
is in the rain. And thus it will be more difficult to hear
who from the rainbow will cry out the tale.

1959   *(WA)*

21

CAPRICORN

Roses of frost burst at the windows, and a world
incredible and empty startles the trees, now
that the insipid tang of snow above the wind
runs in the grey of morning, and the hour
of the skylark is dark, ash-mute, a miraculous
happening buried in thickets and sleep. But see:
sweeter perhaps is the time of apples, more clear
in the burden of the eyelids. Count it a time
when the vision ranges and changes, seeing if still
the invisible roots of dream have scooped out enigmas and tunnels.
In the empty dwelling where rests in silence the sign
of my birth, the years and divinings, a thorn of light
assays the apex, the live apex of waking.
Winter is my infancy and my death.

1959   *(VW)*

TWO FIGURES AT THE DOOR

Of bronze, yes, with the key and the introibo.
Volutes. 'What is it, sir?' There were two, at
the door. Breasts of honey and flaxen hair.
Two at night and time is belched forth.

He went to the door. In the dark
the oleander was a void in the snow. A hand
behind the door, white, called him.
                                        City without terror,
man without terror, indifferent. With these
vague hints and symbols, with these impassioned forms, in the scent
of wet ashes, writing, for them
who have sinned against the light, and for them
who have undone the dark, sinning against the dark,
and this insistent voice that calls
in a silence of ashes, always.

'I have sought stories in every verb
as in every word, but even facts escape, and so
how can we, logically, order these facts?'

He went to the door. In the dark
and in the silence he saw also her face, trembling,
the flaxen hair and only one word
cried in the silence without a sound.

The other was waiting farther behind. Dolcissima. Singing.

1959   *(VW)*

THE NAVIGLIO CANAL AT NIGHT

There is no piety in these parts, and the wisdom
of the old is like a sightless moth, and mine like a cuckoo at prayer
in the silence of this city, when between one cloud and the next a star
writhes and screams, and the fields of green and brown waver in the wind
suspended from iron bridges, and visions appear, broken
by a louder silence, until the cock summons from the darkness
the indifference of the dead, and scatters the living.

1959   *(ME)*

FROM PAVILIONS OF WIND

Is a wheel of flame, a bird, a song or an orchard
of apples the world, and you recognize it, with words wide
heard in the ear when the sky slides
into its ditch of exile.
                            But when
winter calls you, it's too late then to affirm, too
late to refute truth, to destroy traces, to deny
the exhausting act of being a man, with his
intelligent power of muscles and memories.

23

At the intuitive hour
when the moon rises from mirrors and white is slain
and all saints and heroes grope in the sewers and a butterfly's body
scribbles on windows letters of love, all the lives that you havent lived
condense mute and possible in shadowy transit. Burnt.
From the four
pavilions of wind issues one voice, and it's always yours.

1959   *(CC)*

THE ACROBAT

to Vladimir Mayakovsky

Too much time has gone by, as you know,
and Russia is far away. I see you
with your hoop and a mongrel dog who leaps
through the middle of the hoop and into the green
sky of exile — at the first shot,
like the crack of your whip. Amid the crowd
only three women, six men and a boy
take note, between the wall and the night,
of your heroic leap, and your red costume
lifts off with difficulty in the European sky.

1959   *(CW)*

HIBERNATING MAMMALS

to Rodolfo Aricò

When the silence drowns (and in the silence
a silence more piercing, a shriek), then
with the precision of refined cruelty, with the grey
and pink open in an empty space — and again

24

as soon as hibernating mammals, as you may have read, are
subjected to extreme cold, the commerce of their breathing
— or of any other function — dwindles; but with us, and
with you in particular (the straight lines intersecting,
the flight, the sudden spasm . . .)

                 conjecture upon conjecture, a circle,
an engraved sign and a polished pebble
at the troubled centre of your rational mind —
it is only then that your night (and mine,
through cold continuous breathing) is like
the coherent expression of a world grizzled with frost.

1960   *(CW)*

WITH THE SELFSAME SILENCE OF OBJECTS

With the selfsame silence of objects,
                       a moon of virgins, a fountain,
a dove or a cry in the mist
                   of a worn-out door I shall listen
to your footsteps, this last earth
                 of men or desert of streets
making my separation,
                 and I shall read with no fear
'facilis descensus est'
               chiselled into a stone,
a headstone hidden by asphodels.
                 Words of a private message.

Then your refusals will have
               little importance, and little
the hope that I'll recognize you,
                a hope always dismissed.

Shall I change desire, and the evil
                              of unsatisfied desire
for a fist that clenches, contracting
                              on the dust wet with rain?
or change your face for another,
                              a face repeating itself,
transforming useless choice
                              to an anonymous terror?

Come, my lips will say,
                    Come, and I shall follow
my words that descend with myself,
                    and my hand will touch a hand
on my body, a hand I know
                    (where asphodels flower) as my own.
                    Words of a private message.

With the selfsame silence of objects,
                    as I hear your steps on the gravel
grow back into a dull sound
                    of irrevocable decisions,
still in me out of me lives
                    a certainty of love.

              Does my garden give you pleasure?
              The right answer is yes.

1960   *(VW)*

ON THE BANKS OF THE LAMBRO, THINKING OF THE FUNERAL MONUMENT OF GASTON DE FOIX

But when
we are all one, what do we do next? A mass of sounds
twists the madrigal of the skylark, a knot of wind.

              My Lombard river,
curving color of mice and slime, insists on turning brown
in Brianza's green, color
assuming no other, and farther off immured in tedium
nestled amid the teeth of a poppy.

26

                              And green corpses
fall now from the wind, not only birds,
for all the waters must be consumed
before a beginning is possible, until whoever's returned
can still go, and whoever has gone still be troubled.

                              And so,
I dont wake you, stone, nor can I ever awaken you
if Gaston de Foix sleeps in you
almost suspended in air, and breathes the light (death
and nature astonished) of white walls, instrument revealed
and end unknown, where the given can never
know change, and only what is expressed
destroys the appearance of immobility. You therefore
no longer bind me to this earth, faith is destroyed,
an acrid smoke enters my room, poetry has lost
its peculiarity, nothing is left but to wait for the moment
when in the eyesockets eyes again will be seen,
a hand on the shaft of the hand, and out of woman
and man one image alone will be made.
                              The mind disarmed
by a love of stone, see how the song that breaks
rhythms and phrases at a crossing of branches high in the wind, lacks wonder —
                but if the birds bear
on darkened wings that color, their flight no longer's for you.

1960   *(CC)*

A FEW VERSES FOR CHRISTMAS

Where Christmas rose and gladiola meet, the snow
dances from wire to leaf like a blind cat,
and the outskirts, with black hoods and lanterns,
recall the Ripa Ticinese,
                an ancient lay-brother
conceived by the cold, crouched on the house-tops.

27

the dawn is still distant,
the flowers within themselves open new words,
in an art of gesture unknown to me, hidden
in time, and a disorder in which
the fiction of order had long been reason
explodes in the silence.

1960   *(WA)*

CAFÉ MOZART

At Café Mozart seven enamored
        and three young girls, all placed apart,
deluded time when a dark waitress
        with semitic features and laughing eyes
scurried about with Don Giovanni whirled
        from a gramophone.
        Naked, shaggy,
with a Viennese coffee glass
        amid tables and talons
of wrought-iron chairs and consumptive mirrors,
        in the darkness a restless figure hid
who had my thoughts, and let them go
        in the pungent smoke of the last Pall Mall.

1960   *(WA)*

EVEN THE SNOW THEORIZES ITS LAWS

Neither mandrakes nor dolls are found
among these dry lunar shoots by the stream.

Yet other roots, human, sink in the air.

Ecstasy is mobile, the snow
is not in the same spot always and only.

28

Even the snow theorizes its laws.

In this house the fire of your eyes
burns objects and changes perspectives.

Liquids and stones have a definite voice.

In the air's neutrality all the new names
born of this union scoop out the mind.

And a snow of exile nullifies my laws.

1960   *(WA)*

LONGFELLOW'S HOUSE

    The snow had attained
its topmost pedestal and a visionary cock flung
into the violet night its wounded wattles.
                             On a terrain
of leaves and thorns, sepulchred and separate,
Longfellow's house was a preposterous museum
of counterfeit volumes, a garden conquered by crows
and iris
           (juice of the iris, imbibed by the old masters
against ennui and wind):
                     a December lost,
        a perfume
of polluted snow and of éclairs that melt
in the mouth now while I sit to give ear to the rain.
                               Far off,
disguising in me my limited size, I hear that soul and hair
grow like the sum of years in a looking glass.

1961   *(WA)*

THIS REALITY

Yes, I have to confess it, for years now
reality, wearing its ridiculous
cocked hat much like a
character out of Brecht, has nervously
winked at me from corners, but seldom
spoken my language, and assured me
it was not exactly myself.

And now I wonder, observing
photographs and landscapes, clouds and bits
of colored paper, trees, women,
geodes round and red as angry fists
rotating in my eyes, how far this
experience of things whether total and false
— not whether true and partial — goes and I take refuge
in evoking the shades of history
as if they were all (and no one renounces
first person singular) not already the projection
of my conditioned will, but the sum
of what is dead, out of some prophecy.
                                        So,
amid the varying moments of time, in every pause,
where my poetry runs out of breath,
is a ruined threshold, an empty temple
where the wind keeps signalling something.

1961   *(CC)*

EPIGRAM

Aside from art, which is already a long time damned
by chthonic curiosity or indifference,
angels disturb me, though they
do not surprise me when they come
with gifts of perfectly copied waxen-fruit.
As for me, I prefer a worm-eaten apple
to their solemn, supercilious patience.

1964   *(WA)*

THE BLACKBIRD

The last time the snow
dreamed a night as cold as this, the blackbird
imagined he had a nightmare sheen
of polished silences in his throat, and in his wings
time to make himself a starched ruff
like Shakespeare's. His voice fell
from a branch like a shadow, and the air became
a raised pulpit, lifting it higher than its weight.

1964   *(RB, MD)*

THE KINGFISHER

Who in a wingflash I saw
reduce a whole cloud
to a drawing of cloud-section
with segments washed in blue
and the word sky written in Chinese ink
upon the highest limit:
                              I wondered
how he could move through an absciss
on those geometrical heights if the wind
had already decided its direction

1964   *(RB)*

ELEGY FOR VERNON WATKINS

You would have said the hills of Wales
were green and violet in the parched
and ferny sea wind, that harebells
and horses were out, cloud riding,
and gulls and herons hurtled on air
like whitest petals of white flowers.

31

And you would have given yourself up wholly
to the rhythmical, blinding, lullaby chime
of the concave moon and its mirroring sky,
saying, 'This constant signing of tide
on sand, this is my interpreter,
of myself to myself — vision, contemplation,
sound and silence in the perfect accord
of spade and soil, sickle and clover.'
Meanwhile you would watch at your eastern window
the rush of shadow, falling, spreading,
open armed, leaving only in the shell
the last light and the last wound,
holly of memory, before it transformed
into the deep but dazzling darkness.
Others I have abandoned dead
and watched fade, quiet and composed
within living minds only, after death only,
certain we would not betray their lies.
But you saw the gold eyes of birds
immutable in a verb of clear waters
and air a wavering column of meanings
hung between a motionless butterfly
and mystery stilled in its butterfly wings.
So you may spurn our mourning, being completed,
and return smiling, no longer seeking
in the crystal ball you hold in your hands
anything other than its own light and curve
navigating an October dusk. You need yield
no more to nostalgia. The Pennard soil
records your light footstep, your praying step
that made rocks fast and colossal the sea,
all as it should be, blood grain, corn ear,
mating in your step, your breath. Meanwhile
I see you play tennis with Taliesen, backhanding
his serve across the Atlantic. You watch
the imperfect trajectory but pay no heed
if asked to trace on the court of the deep
conscious footprints by correcting your step
or accepting the rules of the game. You would say
there is no contradiction in this immense violet
night blooming out of the sunset
over the hills of Gower with its cold
swan's wings accompanying its wake.

In your bones you knew abstract conjecture
could never yield a true equation. Wholly
for this, perhaps, you return. You achieved a match
between your partial vision and time's limitations
and now have taken back that vision's meaning
into the deep but dazzling darkness.

1967 (RB)

PORTRAIT OF A FRIEND

Crazed, he drinks and eats
nothing of this world. His head in turmoil
spurs him through unmapped lands. With pen
and armchair swivelling, speaking
only in the fourth person singular, he leaps
in the saddle to amble through reflections
and drown in a syllable snare.
                                        Goodbye.

1967 (RB)

FROM THE NOTES OF KEATS BEFORE WRITING THE
ODE TO A NIGHTINGALE

Beneath a plum? Could be. Mr. Brown testifies
as to some papers. Three or four sheets. Illegible script.
A cloud in the Hampstead afternoon
lets loose a spring fluid with sound.
Dryads. Luscinius. A horizontal flight,
a firm, unforeseen detachment where the branches bow
to intersect the shadows. Jug. TWIG.
Twig. twig twig twig. Jug. Say it again
I see a tremulous incense hangs upon the boughs.
TWIG. Deceit oozes from those notes
and the color along the girdling wall
shows yellow cadaverous nuances.

                    Darling,
on the teaspoon a murmurous fly, on the cup's edge
an elegant fiend twists his coat-tails like a jet
of gas. And this, we interpret it how,
master Vellum? Banners. To take a glance
at the Encyclopedia Britannica. And then,
to pose two hours for Severn. I'd like to know
if Mrs. S. still slices butter and bread
with such precision. Look! now
I can even see it. Better castrate,
with a razor, verses like these (or, let us say,
curtail,
            as more proper
for my profile: National Portrait Gallery). Understood,
for abortive poets only. From Margate. Migrant.
Iambic pentameter and aquatic plumage,
shafts and barbs, down, spur, caruncle, slender beak
in conical shape, sternum, and sacs of air
in a requiem turned to sod. Luscinius.
Many a time I have thought of death . . . yet, in fact,
perhaps old Coly is right: only a fixed idea.
'These hoarse unfeather'd Nightingales of Time,' etc.
The feathers flying headlong. Seated. He brought
a breakfast-room chair beneath the plum. Three hours.
Across the engraving of Vivares and Woollett
the light plays on the windows of Claude Lorraine. And then
he placed the scraps in a book with unassuming air. Good,
so it will be said. TWIG. Truly possessed, happy. Pity
it isn't twilight yet. Twig.
Oh to fade far away, dissolve, and quite forget
what you among the leaves have never known, fever,
the weariness and fret, the palsy that shakes
the hair . . . Laughter. Might one through laughter
catch some glimpse of death? The light slants now
toward the other wing of Wentworth Place,
the plaintive anthem fades
in the direction of Margate. Migrant. I should write
to Fanny.

1968   *(WA)*

34

LA FAIBLESSE DE LA RAISON DE L'HOMME

parait bien davantage en ceux
qui ne la connaissent pas qu'en
ceux qui la connaissent

Knowing that flies find reasoning tough
or that a Tyrolean woodpecker's jittery beak
strikes midnight with a computer's meticulous pride
is not enough: ghosts
still use the Gregorian chant, perfect canon
for expression of ancient terrors.
                                        As for me,
I know that since Blake lost his wig
even the compass of God is put in doubt, and this
to me seems a positive good. Only doubt remains
to pay homage to hope.

1968   *(WA)*

TOWARD WINTER

Always in accord with the evil event
the bathroom pipes resound with the tones
of faunlike afternoons, and fear
all awry like a happy mongrel
mimics a squall of ages. Now
I no longer can doubt it: Europe trots
toward winter on a single foot.

1968   *(WA)*

OUR LADY OF KING'S ROAD

Tipsy tubercular filthy louse-blackened
Byzantine madonna, haloed in tatters
smutty postcards and fake flowers,

35

my sad eyed archivist
of the libraries of sleep,
soul lined
in wallpapers of childhood,
anima uagula blandula
maybe, in some acid hallway
green with beer and urine,
who between rolled down tights
keepeth the last sacrament:
now, from this shadow falling
in a sickly flesh-pink,
intercede should some gentle guy
snatch a secret glance at you, and listen
to the fog's footsteps, uneasy virgin,
self-absorbed and veering
along this our king's road,
and pray for the beatles, for the mantises
in the shop-fronts of all the antique dealers,
for a poncho of kneeling Indians
in strawberry fields forever, and respond
to this cold that creeps up from the basement,
interrupting its argument
with your hands soiled by compliance.
Barefoot, pray
for us also
now, and at the hour of our lives.

1968   *(RB)*

ALTEREGO

Alterego, mocking face, fluttery docent
in long lightgray dresscoat, my old
philistine master of silences inserts
his profile in tricks of infallible mirrors, quick
insinuates little hands in an opaque silver
and from it extracts
miniscule hollow souls, frail
sprigs ripped from the elder dripping

pale violet ink, an archive
of obsessive analogies. The es-sense,
the id-entity is organized in automata that get
resolved in references, allusions, flowery
quotes and comments as footnotes. At mysterious
sounds and signals the academic hair
is ruffled, logical consequence, is tossed
by invisible organs. Old
Alterego, choirmaster,
candidly sneers in a book of violent snow.

1969 (CC)

REGULAE AD DIRECTIONEM INGENII

To pour on a little cube of petrarch
an iodic drop of angostura. To write 'end'
in English on the wooden horizon
of dead western nature, and then
to watch the monk wind rise in its saffron dress,
and to sketch insects in the uncertain mesopotamia
between the Ticino and banks of the Po.
                                    Slowly
to chew two nails,
to gaze at length on the empty pupils
of a potsherd head and to swallow
the insipid insolence of the inferno,
the syncope,
the obscene dance in a ring
of the termites on top of the bookcase. And to persist
in saying 'tu' to Nefertiti. We shall see.

1969 (WA)

ZIGGURAT

Eminent singer Ur-Nina with the ambiguous boon
of crossed legs on rugged pyramids
transforms even his voice.

They laugh,
the hummingbirds of stone, trilling a canon
of ill-famed gaieties, and at the horizon
earth's arid river grows round, the night, austere
twist of the shadows, solemn coleopterans that scale the wind,
the steps, the voice of Ur-Nina,
and they dissolve in coituses of sand.

Already yesterday, tomorrow, beyond.

1969   *(WA)*

VAUCLUSE

even style sometimes can overwhelm
the description of a river or mirror
where the wind of evening sails
in an utterly blameless green,
                              but
even if no time were left between the deeds and words
to intuit the avalanche when the lavender seed grows,
or to make out icebergs in the dew,
                                        even if
of no use the wretched room
beneath the rock, the manuscripts and album
of touristical-poetic signatures,
                those we love will live a long time,
                will live
to ask themselves with me the meaning
of this survival defended till the last
                perhaps,

                here where redbreasts abound,
                where icy water
                carries among the leaves a time
                always older and more clear than a memory;

those we love will still live a long time
drinking at subterranean fountains

1969   *(WA)*

PARK HOTEL

It was that point in the night when whisky melts
into multiple blunt voices speaking from sacks
of soiled linen, when rain like raucous equilibrists
crackles from a record. By a stream a skylight of willows,
and a man rows with the herbage as far as the groin,
pulses strain toward the light: in the longing of waters
a girl in pallid whites reflects long eyes
of farewell where her open dress
insinuates serene fevers.
                         A burning candle
among curled-up socks. The things that kill. The soles
of yellow feet beneath the blankets. A basket
of opaque plastic in silence, an Empire sink
on a spiral solumn. Deodorants and mirror, stools
where cigarettes have burnt the glaze
on linen towels: ubi oculos
ubi amor,
                and a cracked old bidet, an odor, acute,
of brothel where on the ceiling in sad stillness
nymphs and goats play.
                         The sorceress
has not spoken.
                Do not expect anything
from this explanation, the ideas unravel
like the feces of fish, the moon
wavers at the windows, rain stiffens the memory
and the man rows with the herbage as far as the groin
where the dream traverses
the purple moquette of sighs.
I could tell you that time brightens like foam,
or that an eleatic old man debates
the truth of the marks you left
on the cushion beside my neck, doubting
that you believe yourself a flamingo's equal,
but only this liquor of words is true
when the night is displaced to deny you.

1970   *(WA)*

39

APRIL

Let us not confute the water,
nor the dripping benedictine plant
on the clouds' azure coasts,
nor jargon scraping in turkeys' throats,
nor a slimy carp's tail among seaweed,
    so slow, bursting
into a bubble of dissolving eyes, black eggs,
   but
     — and instead —
springtides on stilts of glass, backward
and imponderable articles of faith
with all their sounds that betray
the consequentia rerum.
       They are not enough,
those Linnaean names impaled by pins
at a flower's core, near pale petals
from which in the niche of one's eyes
music ascends, to be sure
April is the month that returns
with imperfection and tender leaves,
with tender wishes, embraces that linger,
     suspended, in the gleam
of your hoarse dark voice,
       saying
the new season will bear the trace
of a milky way that is silent and bright
in the grooves of the hand in mine.
       Walking
the confines of the pristine trauma,
let us not confute the water,
nor the liquid transparent plant,
but only our own discordant step,
faithless as an anemone nosegay forced
      out of season.

1970   *(WA)*

FOR AN ATLAS OF DESCRIPTIVE ANATOMY

Stereotaxis: it could also be
an allegory if all these colored charts,
swollen and lifelike, did not leak
on the feet of an old inebriate,

so that horizons rise on high, deserts,
above the stunted cypress of the memory,

and the Macaca Fuskata Kusama studied,
the Japanese monkey that mimes
anthropoid geographies with his brain,
writes frenetic letters of love.
                              On the skull
alphabets of insomnia conclude
cycles of civilization, and on unaccustomed lines
there twists the light reflected
from speechless scraps of guttural iron.

                              Morning
cracks open in the east like a papaya.

1970   *(WA)*

IN CONSEQUENCE

Who will be able to find me again
in this corner, fly or baboon, twilight
or saint, by this idle hill
brimming with gods, with vines
and crossword puzzles restored
to the sudden, clearly cut smile
of spring? Spitting from a tower
seeds of crackling logos, weaver birds
draw lines and dig from the air
a profile of memorial stone. There is nothing
I can redeem. A blade of lucern bores spots
of sun on the crust of my hair. Corner
not of my birth. Again. In consequence.

1970   *(WA)*

41

A DOUBT

Rule to itself and to falsehood, a bronze tree
strips itself in silence between the hoofs
or upon the sluggish spine of a rhinoceros,
      where
signs carved centuries ago bring back
unconcluded histories.
      And yet,
let us suppose it defined
by objects known with certainty:

    what else could Descartes say?

1970   *(WA)*

THESIS

but the day they will find me again, should they find me again,
to think, in the shade,
should a shade be possible — and not, surely, the third one,
the shadow which more or less should walk at our side —
to think what it was (diabolum) that pushed me once
to the Lambro as if to the Liffey, fanatic, or to the knight
as to a knight, the sword and all the rest (the beard, I say),
dignitate mortis included, which is, all know,
a posthumous attribute, a necessary lyric repose,
parenthesis, or wedge or momentary decline one mocks
through stylistic need (the fact
that even the eternal father is a poet
is not enough to convince me fully),
let me be given license
of another nature, bio and degradient:
to add my obulus thereto

1970   *(WA)*

RECITATIVE

followed by little pucks who deceive you,
who bite through to your blood,
who are not fires but frozen, feline,
shaggy elves between custom and dream,
laughing (there are worse things than thought),
and when you wake, your memory gone,
soft mulberry leaves grow upon you / where? /
and in the distance strange
and varied noises, they flame / a comedy / and you
could wear all the clothes you wish — others
there are who weave still other desires
in you — deceive you, and a long
long white hand which you feel
anxiously gropes in the armchair padding /
from nothing nothing can come, he said /
and on you they put soft pointed hats: the pirouette
would be uncomely, would cut in two parts
the time, which you instead bite, the skin and all,
watching yourself in the mirror / surround
yourself with sleep if you wish better to know,
not the nature of dreams, but the nature of that,
in fact, which you hold in your fist / a clod
of earth / yourself curtailing the scene,
having time no more to discuss
the desolation out of which
another act can again begin,
if it is true that the theater begins
with a man who walks in thought
across a darkened stage / and you:
watch him / and then? /
followed by little pucks you only deceive
the minds of moonstruck mules

1970   *(WA)*

OPEN THE DOOR

Open the door, the verse, the wood closet,
the maze, the spider's web,
the myrtle, the mouth,
            and meet a worn out black,
a fossil with poisonous needles,
and stumps, cords, poles to bound the sky,
                                    this
responsible, irresponsible hybrid
of many endeavors natura naturans has not ended
as god's ecological tracts proclaim,
where October rust on the maples
exfoliates in foaming mutations, ecstasy
and excrement of pigeons in a wind
that vomits velvets on the face of the evening;
and it is this you see, shops of dust,
accountings and low temptations, arms,
chairs moulded by moss, furloughs,
final struggles with death.
                        Open, then,
the door, the earth; the earth, *aside*
as in an Elizabethan monologue.

1971   *(WA)*

DESERT,

        celebration
of the other side plus prophetic stammering
            muffled
gaps in all the words
whoever is called on to utter
                    will never be able to read

    (with infinite patience, the future,
an upright figure in absence,
crumbles between the teeth
of an unknown Ezekiel)

44

                    still, in spite of everything
there is the attempt at unity,
geometrical nowhere of always
the colour of polished jade
to us, who want to prolong it — and we
plod on, in illusion of the immediate
                    not forgetting
that only the finite has an exit

1971   *(RB)*

LITTLE MOUNTAIN LANDSCAPE

On the summit a drizzle of rusted trees
and the snow,
                    my writing scratched in the snow
by a dog's back paws,
                    runs through the gorges, artifice,
the deceitful equestrian tricks
of alphabets in the optics of a hawk,
                    and a cloud dangles
in the thrilling of the firs.
                              Yes, in the spring
this mountain was a fish, it flew,
            unnatural
naturalness of nature that disseminates itself
playing the mad poet's part.

1971   *(WA)*

JOURNEY TOWARD THE NORTH

Lichen, moss, trolls, arguments
of ancient salt-encrusted casks,
                              and conifers, maybe,
marching upon a granitic pack in the gulf stream, past
the arctic circle of your eyes.

And again: gneiss, time overturned,
saltations of the bust, opposition of the head,
the cloud that swells the circumference of the arms
around the solemn face, the nights that lie beneath settling down
with the color of dusk.
Hypnosis.
And the distances
diminish — the foot on the stairs, the door,
her glance.
The journey has been long. I know.
You have surmounted the burnished walls
of extinction and ecstasy,
the tombs in the shape of women,
the tara
of serene green bronze, and you have smothered the cry
of the nimble pollulant uroboros. The roots
and circular flight of the wind have touched
the grain that sprouted already
in your hair.
I insist.
You lose yourself in a rose
like a sherpa in an isle. Salt and mould. Butterflies
like shoals of herring quiver through the depths
of your voice.
And patiently you bind, cultivate
and protect the pollen and ashes.
A dense perfume
of violet air and organisms in the livid margin
of moraines, crevices, regurgitation of breaths, queries
(and unbroken sounds: 'to dare to fall asleep,
the dog between your legs'), and in the smoke
— the peat, the waters —
the latitude north at 68 degrees.
Down there, where the cold
sometimes stammers at the snow bunting's bony splash
and cuts, for an instant only,
with a feigned springtime the fixed horizon
in the pupils, I ask you,
overturning
per aspera ad astrid the lands
where remote gulls pierce with their beaks
a long-shadowed maelstrom,

                              what thing, what words
rip the Lofoton to the reverberation
of your silences?
                              The snow
has violet striations, footprints appear, the birds
form low-flying columns with strident notes
along the perfection of the glance, fingers
flutter on the snow.
                              Insensibly
shapes like bedspreads of white wolves
beckon you from a wall of clouds,
or crippled enigmatic smiles, on which fear
is put to rest. Difficult
to awaken all the way to you.

1971   *(WA)*

LETTER I

The word that follows the word,
    the green
leash holding the fish by the tail,
                the glove
over eyes that rummage among grass,
    thumb
probing for the gift of the round
        stone,
                and the waning
light that plucks the word
    out of a circle of rain —
                            these
chance occurrences do not connect
        show
no affinity, yet
surfaces flicker,
                set,
                    spread rays:

47

a mould
on graves humanly and
perhaps the sole intruder

I find
myself in a gust of wind

1971   *(RB, MD)*

LETTER II

skull bones damaged by
a lunatic genitive, with
a hole in the middle, perfect,
so that through it god
may spit his grace on us

1971   *(RB, MD)*

LETTER IV

in fine style,
in the sense
that the soul
has neither curves
nor triangles
or rather no
pirandellian algae

for which reason we say
that in the land of the knowing rat
there is no greenness other than that
spreading out of his tail

in fact, in the absolute
nothing exists

1971   *(RB, MD)*

LETTER VI

To Guido

The sharp tip of a shoot
  pricks the soles of our feet.
We get ready for a night of voices
  with breathless slowness, watching
our remains wrapped up in a sheet,
    through the arch
of a door swarming with signs,
    with insects,
      with black crumbs.

We shall dig tongues out
        of desert mouths.

1971   *(RB, MD)*

LETTER VII

Muddy light,
        autumn,
              dahlias swelling
obscene beneath the wall, tortured
by a poisonous yellow.
              Like a sadist
I watch an upturned black
beetle's scrabbling legs.

  Thus, having proved
I exist, or believe I exist,
I rummage with a stick in the folds
of appearances, I turn up ideas, I rake
myself like a lousy springtime, I shove
everything back to its origins.

49

In the end, among strands of hair,
I shall find myself a word of grass.

The dahlias
    devour the light, they close over
the beetle-legged pistil.
    Autumn has dissolved
        in a crack in the wall.

Thus, having proved
I exist, or believe I exist,
        writing,
I follow attentively the black
silent scrabbling of words.

1972   *(RB, MD)*

THE STORY LOST IN THE SNOW

give me time, a time that reverberates, and you
at the center
    empty air, mangled phantoms, white hollow
from sunken tracks of scornful bears, and a thread
of gelid slaver vibrates from villous slopes,
    other shapes pursue each other in silence
    around the queen,
    culpably,
and for snouts and noses masks (yes)
                a sunset livid
as a snowdrop, and I,
hearing the rotted mandibles gnawing
the buried herb-leaves, the chestnut bits, mountains
in kitchens of the Domenicans, where snow
and the raven nest among branches, I,
                looking
into fires of the hearth, have hidden words in the ashes,
                under
            that gray where winter

              crackles —
                        here should be wind
on the moors and a lunatic vagrant, whose
jaws hang on a black cape, tac
tac his stick on the ice
                        here should be cries
in the distance and closing doors,
transferable forests and coffee dregs
in this design of white dogs who run in the white
                        — I allow myself only to hear
the rigorous stutter of space, the stars
contorted, surmised...
ah, a handsome contrivance death, first rate
instruction, ask the lame man's stick
what the weather will be,
                        mangled phantoms,
                                and a woman
with gray eyes now sits on my lap, a woman,
     her hands,
no need of five fingers
to put to death your king, fear is
an indecent invention,
                        her hands on her mouth
for some inconceivable shame,
                        'sin is
no more than a theological thing,' is this
what she wished to impart to me?
                        behind my ear the Grecian grief
of the crows while I dig a darksome name
from those brunhildish ashes, and a fan
formed like a fox from the streams, out there,
waves yes to me with its tail,
                        and at once I recall
how morning's archeology is pink,
that definitive moment that wavers
between the shadow of one's hair and the longest
figure on the horizon

1972   (WA)

51

FROM A CONVERSATION BETWEEN HERMES AND
MENIPEUS ON A FIELD OF SNOW

'but our subconscious is foxy...'

So, it is natural enough,
infinite excuses are found for one's life, fate,
Gallup polls, chance, cartilages irritated
in the nasal septum, ancient ordinances
from above, and most of them agreeably mysterious,
as if the rain sufficed to set history aright, smiles
of potsherd hung on the trees.
                                        The snow,
          askew, white,
and in the background walls of mist, and only, sometimes,
something that rolls, scratches, shrieks,
a sort of music that rips
this frame that fascinates poets (Hermes
to Menipeus: the bones), this pallid void
of baptismal fonts, scars, origins,
odors of burning juniper, incense, and always
allusions like dangling sleeves, the arms forgotten,
elsewhere, not even swollen with wind, no,
not even this vileness of putrescent saints, of ex-votoes
in the ice-cold crackling air.
                                        Life
and its myriad apologies. Yet art
has no loop-holes. Balanced atop
a Flemish floor in perspective
a pensive spider with eyes of a fox
directs its nape and bishop, which cross
at a sensitive point, at the center,
fraudulent relations. Nothing? A void?
And to say the Pythians claim wages
even for forecasts of misfortune.
                                        All right, then,
better to pull the plug, to break
the celestial circuit, the contact,
to sit without motion watching the snow
that climbs and twists about a broom in the valley, higher
than the reddened hands with which you are composing, always,
your portrait.

1972
                                                        (WA)

THE LOVE-LETTER OF THE MAD GARDENER
HANS BREITTMAYER

Unity and dispersion. We should part.
On a wall painted yellow a wandering passion
of granular shadows. Perhaps it is also
the remains of a meal. Brutal
ineffable push of thought on the word.
And not even an image, an ongoing life
of losses. Disorder. With a wooden door
that affirms an organized void. And with nothing to say
the tension gives rise to the more genuine right,
to birth, things, fragments. Yes,
we should part. Equilateral.

1972   *(WA)*

WAR CORRESPONDENCE

There was nothing but mud all over. The lice
    left visible imprints.
Someone with an open mess-tin between his legs
said / lads, this is bloody farcical / and
    the sentry to the cavalry
        spat a Chinese ideogram,
                                older
than General Giap, and still quite incomprehensible
to anyone with different tastes.
                        On the other side, far off,
A sudden thump answered. Crack.
    It started to rain again.

1972   *(RB)*

53

WHERE

Where April, with all
the superstitions sown by autumn
stays perched on the flank
of the snow for months, for years,
    fretted
by a beech branch, and hoarse
as a fox,
        I am told
the rascal nightingale used to nest
in a mesh of silvers and mosses,
hooded by toadstools
in the ochre thicket, at sunset,
stunning passers-by with his whistle.
    Between one note and another
a tiny sleigh runs across your little toe.

1972   *(RB, MD)*

THAT BEING HAS REPRESENTATIONS ISN'T THE PROBLEM, IT'S THE FACT

There are no functions
    (in a sense), and
light is not if not from stone to stone
        seeking
the body's degradation, the proportion
of the complexity, where a word
        rattles, phallus,
and the sound regenerating / this
representing against all certainty,
        illegal
science establishing the deception
        of the eyes

1972   *(CC)*

54

WINTER PLACES

Winter places,
    those you are familiar with and those
pitifully, you've had described to you,
       which you know
you couldn't celebrate, with a handful
of wild rose hips, or in ancient sandstone,
    your orders being to stretch yourself
as if you were a theorem (sooner or later
    encompassing the present),
                in this cold
I can't define them, either with my passion
    or with my denial;
       snouts of fishes in a sleep
of running waters, they're completely uncontrollable,
    they keep moving, somersaulting
and turning their backs, even though confined
within the very words that are derived from them,
    you cynical old character
       living in a skull case

1973   *(RB)*

MIND-EASER / PSYCHO-TONIC

    We listen to
moving slow behind the eyes the signs
of a barren countryside. In the air
meditated phrases flatten out. You've broken
meaning like bread, repeated the philosophical
monk seated on a jagged rock.
Unattainable green work — coming down
where a snake dies in the grass,
    and every thing
gravitates about the belly; there is no
dictionary of the body, architecture
camouflaged by fear, and nevertheless
this sinister rustling is creative.

1973   *(CC)*

55

POETRY DOES NOT IMPROVE WITH THE YEARS

... the rubbish, crutches, chagrin, road to Calvary,
palimpsests of reason, Erasmian follies,
dramatis personae darling revelling
in shabby ideas worn thin in barrack-rooms,
lice of one's forefathers, and the monologues...

even if one wanted to dwell on the pity and dust
layered up by wind and circumstance
between an elegiac and a Seneca, or the readiness
to haul life squarely on one's shoulders, and shake off
all the ills of writing

... and the wrinkles and the faeces and the sinnings,
the stinking moods and festering loves and faux pas,
old jokers with swollen noses and words minced up
and depressions oh dialectical — shivering
psychiatrists shipwrecked off Cape Horn
centuries back
        the fact remains
not one of these is acceptable
justification   our hair
falls out first
       one supple-jointed
morning of solar visions, ta ra toot toot,
in crazy blackbirds' beaks, of starry eyes,
of minty taste in gardens
drenched in rain and good intentions — you never know
when it will all burst into flower
          ... and the legs
spread wide, policeman's whistles, regrets, reproaches, sands
of history, gossip, guessings, goadings, nails
that never scratch a single thought, tongue that never
knocks once on conscience...
       if it is true you only notice
life by taking a look at yourself in the mirror
poetry does not improve with the years

1973   *(RB)*

FIGURE (I)

If a figure contains a space, it surely reaches
its own limits —
                    that tabby in the garden, for example,
unravelling the ibis redibis with its sharp claws
is watching, lost
in contemplation of the flight,
the arching grace of sparrows, and only one
lets itself be drawn;
                    and so
an outline takes shape, within the body of air,
a perforation of lines, walled in
        by this summer haze

1973   (RB, MD)

FIGURE (II)

the error of an ending does not repeat itself
        at both ends
            of an object
                    (to intuit
that a cloud is square or an anteater is rooting about
sets us free from all limitations);
        what love I bear you, missing
        your closeness, and the way your geisha face
        slopes downwards into shadow
        are wholly personal effects:
            so on again sails
the fleet of the senses, the crisis of autumn

1973   (RB, MD)

A PROPOS OF CHILDHOOD

...rats left long blue parentheses;
they threw off tail-rigging on noisy jetties of grass,
and the night rippled, the third movement
proceeded straight for the shadowy gap
like a tear in a billiard cloth,
and the time developed in 'me' Major dissolved,
swelled, flowed in the rain urged back
on the river ceiling (beneath it some hair made its way
relentlessly, knitted by a drowsy mongrel
bitch) (her name was Beauty),
and he was walking paths of crumbled leaves
with great pearls on a steel nose, he changed direction
with the humid air from the mouth's gaping chasm
while I struggled to decipher the names of characters
in this sort of fable, (his eyes had lost their brows
through overexposure) (how many melancholy moods
I've glimpsed, they cut like the nails of a Bali
dancer in a corner of Fantomas, they slid — screech —
along the silk) (I ran to shut myself in the illusion of an elbow),
fur-lined words of malice bit me and
then left suddenly for the paths of exile, sleep,
leaving me behind to swallow the joys of fear...

1973   (GD, MS)

HISTORICAL COURSES AND RECOURSES

more than once I've heard them laugh

they set out monkey hairs on liberty drapes,
steal gloves with ichthyosaurus eyes (the sea
celebrates its childhood on fossil roots), they carry
in their mouths writing stones,
and tending towards obesity they pack the air's glass panes
in wooden crates, produce straw sounds

(Diogenes circles the agora,
           cynically,
     pulling a dead herring on a leash) —

                              snow
on the negative leaves traces of poison, and we
sling a ladder on our back,
we walk light-stepped,
we don't disturb the rustle that sneaks
past the ageing gaze of springtime,
we bind to the post the impossible clue:

the truth they still propose to us
is nothing but a perfect crime

1973   *(MS)*

LETTER IX

                              forgive me
for mentioning it   the wind has a strange colour
over open eyes   and yet you reject
the only solution, the ferry   death as barking hound
is an entirely predictable figure   slither
a finger over the varnish, compose
alphabets of gestures   split them up   deny them
     how many times have we deceived ourselves
     how many times have we set out —
                              the writing
   sails on gracelessly, and still
     no shadows spread
        by any secret mechanism: we are those
emancipated from sleep   unskilled   arguing only
what route a straight line follows (the whys, wherefores,
who to blame, the consequences, the judges)   we have
   left the job to life
     midnight laughs through our mouths

1973   *(RB, MD)*

59

CONTINUOUS PRACTICE

Just think, if we had nothing better to do,
if in fact nothing else were left to us
but registering the cold, hammering verbs onto time,
trying to distinguish a spade from a wounded bulb,
digging up a corpse with no biographical concerns,
defining textual meaning (pirots
kirulize elatically, was what I thought it said),
and always unsure of a response should we declare
that two boys were flying arm in arm
among the nymphs, drifting in and out of cloudbanks,
each time with more arms, more legs, more fingers —
then it would all be irrelevant, a constant buzz
or itch, neither map nor territory, the whole practice
of this irritation

1974   *(RB)*

ON THE CHANCE RECOVERY OF A PORTRAIT AT SCHLOSS
LEOPOLDSKRON

it was in lasting grace
I watched you, and the lake was ice,
stone skaters on their hands, windows closed,
the trunk of a lime on the surface
now recovered/
                    we finally distinguished
the last labyrinth, deciphered the moment to tear out
the intermittences du coeur, and suddenly the voice
grew sharper, the story recommenced
with this character/

        your picture
        would still have deceived me:

and it made no sense, it was snow, and yet the style
revealed itself in sums of words. My thoughts

were elsewhere, elsewhere, elsewhere:
                                        the scissors, the smile, a rose
on a country bush, a spectacle, a universe of impotence
that merits faith, or:
                              the fold of the mouth, the Jewish
nose with nocturnal blackbirds groping
among word-endings gone mad, brackets detaching space
from this cold to the place where pitying fragments
of your loud voice drop
to the twisting grass
                        — rest on the light
that wisely slides, dying, dying,
imitation and superimposition, twilight/
                                          perhaps
you wished to tell me of some restless moon on velvet,
of few loves left between the lashes
of cold threads like when it snows/
                                      you were a symptom
of abandonment and return, but it is not to you I write:

move your portrait from room to room, turn it over
on the wall, avoid telling me about it, and revenge
the clever mechanics of silence, the trace
of white on the letter sent,
as we will one day know, to an unknown sender.

1975   *(MS)*

IN THE HOUSE OF THE DEAF

...in the house of the deaf
    they are talking strange dialects,
        they are painting a clavichord black,
they are shouting, and you can't hear them, even if a word
    detaches itself from a dung heap —
                                        the only word
    you register is the one you don't understand:
they rob you of your thoughts — it's only something beating
and rustling deeper down, among the roots, when you cock an ear

61

towards where you are speaking and they are thinking, at the end
of a corridor of vertical earth —

                        what is it they are saying
over and over again, in the house of the deaf,
between the sound and the instrument,

                                  in harmony...

1975   *(RB)*

TO FRANCES RICHARDS, PAINTER

bright in the wake
of a Nazarene Blake
silent angels' corollas wheel
around eyes of air, in a fine spray
from your secret garden,
             until they dissolve away
in a tracery of bewildered lilies;

and in the passion
flowers' passion,
yellow you crucify — as if death
were a blown pollen, a winter birth,
where, innocent
             blooms, they vapour away
ambiguous in a white light's petals.

1976   *(RB)*

LETTER FRAGMENT, TO OSIP

...thinking of the fall, of exile,
it occurred to me, one evening
of pikes reflecting like fireflies in the icy
lenses of my spectacles, to type you a letter
scrabbling among the keys of an underwood carcase,

62

but
without even knowing what I was looking for
in that blackened machinery, among the undergrowth of all
those words, with frantic hand...
(it was cold, and the mist
was wafting over your lamp, winter's green apples were ripening
and straw crunched underfoot, a rusty tongue in the shadows
squirmed among too many 'no comments', and on your knees
you had small snow patches, while over your watch chain
tristia clambered, as the wind clambers...)
I could not go on writing...
people like you are always going off somewhere in a long coat
leaving behind few traces, and a life
comfortless, you might say, as the back of a donkey...
later
I ask myself if it's the air which carries
this strange persistent perfume into the corners
of conscience:
there's no exit from it
and it's very hard to enter

1976   *(RB)*

WELL, FORGIVE ME

well, forgive me, but after so many years
of gobs in the pond
(the surface crinkles, look,
in a kind of smile),
and of plunges,
of grocks
who tumble on my tongue, by fits and jerks, and burn, or else
saints that dwindle on pasteboard deserts,
the more exasperated cravings of corpses propped in chairs,
in brief, after frowns,
oscillations and jocosities
— I know, you are sensitive: but don't take offence —
I forget when I first learned
to drag my lips

over the rough sides of principles
or nail errors in the breasts of dolls,
                    to the end
of compelling them, cynically, to swallow back
    the amazement of snow;
but I've a good idea it was when, with a grimace
that was no longer mine, I began to scratch
a postcard of Heidelberg, that squealed,
                    under the pin,
    obscenely,
                    and alleged apparitions,
    nostalgias,
                    regurgitations:
inadmissible morbidities;
                    in fact, that was the moment
when having you solely because I'd never forced you to stay
struck me as masochism —
                    if I look after you now, my pet,
it's as a demented fly dashing itself time and again against the walls,
    and nobody knows if the cause is boredom, agony or joy.

1976   *(ME)*

ON HOW WE SHOULD ABANDON WITHOUT REGRET ONLY
THOSE THINGS WHICH HAVE COME OUT PERFECT

who the hell are you   what do you want   the line
stretches from one end to the other and also, at a certain point
crosses the mons Veneris   et in nebulas
the resemblance   (but it is always only on a face,
on a leg, on a light, that you are moved to desire,
narcissus, the image)   hers (yours)   and similar things
belonging to mysterious women   the one who pursues you in pink
and black   'who can't quite see what it is
who can't quite see'   there should be no limits
to desperation or to yourself if it were true
    (the mouth wide open, silence)
        that only by crossing over me
can you see that I am lost   and the water like a bed

1977   *(MS)*

64

HUMORESQUE

between suicide and rebirth: yes,
  he convinces me, to keep becoming
more simple and straightforward; but
I sit down under a lime tree — a sort of lingam — and think,
I see a bird and the porcelain air and
he beats his wings, he tears
his tunic on the brambles, the yellow flowers, in the cold
and looks at me, whistles, bobs his head in a showcase
of grey evening;
                    I find this connotation
repugnant, he
only sees nouns I think;
                    and I think,
still life, for example, and the crooked
bend in the path on the rock, in the evening
and I move my foot, the gravel crunches
a crow stumbles and I begin to laugh (it was
a crow, really);
                    and in short,
private business: boredom, the dragging
on of life; but who cares? look,
a cloud passes in the shape of a pistol, and click,
you don't even have time to spit

Swansea, April 1977   *(MS)*

LOSS

is nothing but a second acquisition

ultimately, despite this rain
that slides hunchbacked, distracted, in profile, and tries
to edge its way between sounds
and a glance, between the wisteria and pain,
what the sense can be
of this thing, this shadow, this twisting knot
you will only know when you accept
the spiteful insistence by means of which I am

1977   *(MS)*

BEEHIVE: ENVOI

to Graham Sutherland

this beehive which is crumbling, dust now, with
leavings of pollen perhaps, empty,
                              goes on
relentlessly buzzing, swarming, a frenzied yellow
droning of loss — it is body, a sham, a
                              derelict shell that
stirs up hollow sounds, and sometimes, inside it,
eyes roll back suddenly, and poison flows after poison:
just as, elsewhere at another time, desire
steals into the ever-shifting place:
                              old age
draws back into itself, infinite future stumbling
into a box of shadows

1977   *(CW)*

THE SUSPECT JOY OF THINKING

(it seems) these voids of sound, these rough particles
    of tainted earth
    excite the mind to higher things;
                              and yet
between you asleep and time flowing,
    dissolving,
        and me having stopped writing,
    although I'm writing this,
        and this air crackling
along a grave to articulate a name,
    I rack my brains and stand enraptured,
        I bite my thumbs
                              down
passionate indifference —

66

to descend once more, I tell you,
into the suspect joy of thinking —

but I always
miss the thing in question:
only what is left is improbable
what is

1977   *(MS)*

PARABLE OF WHITE

Yo me sucedo a mi mismo
Lope de Vega

light in the form of a figure. but
all that white tucked neatly away in the cupboard,
immaculate and untouched in a somewhat lugubrious *mise en scène*
of miaows and lace, of death rattles and fingernails, of ever so delicate
petals and chaste triumphs of virtue, suspect lumps,
cluttered malaise and shadows, where words shrivel up,
where sacristies creak and the raven hairs of elderly housekeepers
entwine, in short it pushes mindlessly through,
although it is white, and it raves, it creeps, it whispers, you hear
it demand its opposite, an oilskin, a casing,
and it swells, an organism, it gives birth to signs and Flemish
flowers,
        while she lies under the divan as languid as a moth,
boiserie with the prescribed profile, Louis XIII nymph and suchlike,
and it is only through this she can say she has found herself, identical, other,
with the pressure that finally lays open a life
so unthinkably different, and that is to say the door (before), or the something
in the cupboard that contains her, to flow back
straining yet happy, into the nomadic formulation
of her own existence, which...
                        but then it would be better
to stop stirring up the dilemma of slaked lime,
gazing fondly at the bait if, uncaring
for the object it drowns in, it moves, opens/closes,

67

and returns to what it was,
                           white, light,
where only the sign is in the plural,
      constantly misled by the act of writing

1977   *(MS)*

LADY ABLE

      all the same,
if you happen to fall foul down some parenthesis
left unguarded and meet Lady Able, expert
masseuse of guilts and frustrations, typical
ailments of middle age, do not surrender
to her perfect French:
                           the subtle malice
she wets her lips with, the insinuating delicacy
of her shunting hands, the moist strokes,
render your hopes of eventual relief
into cold hissings and stranger variations; an acrid smoke
dries her tongue between the teeth, a smear of transvestite
eye-shadow trickles between them
                              (do you see how death
                                waggles its hips?)

1977   *(RB, MD)*

THE VISIT

to Ugo Mulas

one of these days of ill omen, a friend
warden of clods, of neoclassical
opuscules, of skulls, a sort
of gardener if one could avoid the image
of a nature made orderly, of hoer,

68

melancholy, odd, with an air of having, some while ago, died,
a fragment of sphinx in his eye,
crumbling between his fingers a chrysalis
case, I became aware
that he had dropped by to see me, absorbed
in some chaste murmuring, I imagine, in connection
with ecpyrosis, kalùga, ragnarök, uncertain
definitions, as always, for all their limpidity,
and dodging the wooden column with the black-looking
sparrow and the gear wheels dangling on threads,
fearful of the stumble and the provocation
of perverse wobblings and tintinnabulations,
he left me a photograph, a quivering
flight of shadow clouds, almost
a piece of sky stippled with smears, with sacred
excrement, and a line of herms, of immobile steles, one
alone with a finger raised level with the lips, the breast
granular, and a lion on the background, in perspective,
so I wonder, whether this change in the light,
unforeseen, may not be a sign — what of
I couldn't say, but at some point life
begins, apparently, crawling again,
like a cheerful grub

1977   *(ME)*

TOWARDS THE CROSSING

Along the laddered water... and a taste for mud is phrased
in the dark cry of the duck, the river weaves
and gathers beneath a white stone fallen from the sky, leaves
brush the brown/blue feathers. I wait, amazed,

and listen to the old ones whisper and dream their dreams
of the Acts of the Apostles, and occasionally strain
mid-stream with a push of their poles, out of winding seams
and fragments of light, of dark; they do not even feign

sleep. Now as I land and think of them, I feel
there must have been a fishes' workshop hidden there below
governed by clockwork crumbs of *selbst*, a wheel

of madly shifting anagrams on dead men's names as when a patrol
passes — some blind Austro-Hungarian exciseman. Only as a foe
do you in fact emerge — in opposition — to pay your ridiculous toll.

1977   *(MS)*

IF

if the great freeze were no more than a sheep, or bone
on which a single codex skated expertly, if
natural mercy could justify ashes,
and unnatural death the anguish of a scream,
if art were painless, madame, as a lover's bite
in the neck, a pleasant stopping place, then nothing
could warn us in advance of the systematic treachery
our difference imposes on us, every time: we would be
the clumsy double of a finitude, the bag
the clown wraps around his head

1978   *(RB, MD)*

THE MOZART FAMILY, 1780/81

what might descend, by way of expression,
from the hazard of notes effusing beyond their staves,
or the drowning of the Mozart family
in the piece for four hands on the spinet, or the violin's dive
down a mallard's guffaw by a colour of rain
enclosed in the picture-frame and hung up to dry,
would perhaps be a keener reflection on the ribbon
pinching the peruke, on the faded rose
where the bourgeois humiliation of music is graciously masked,

if the quill slipped behind the ear of the unquiet shadow
bowed over the ledger of the lakes, did not impose,
by association, motivations to form —
    by choice, and not chance, the room
where everything is enclosed reverberates, unsurprised, the profile
of the young maestro: without collusion it would be unheard of,
his stupefaction.

1978   *(ME)*

VARIATION ON THE THEME,
'WEEPS ON THE DESERT OCHRE AND THE SALT'

The man who built the pyramids had a prominent nose,
and for a model, shadow.
                    He feared the breathings of the wind,
the meticulous triturations of insects, the reverberation
of solemn scaleni. A smile
would barely sever his lips off-screen, he would photograph
six points out of focus between apex and palm-tree,
whose key he held fast.
                    The line taut, the diameter
would fall plumb on each hieroglyphic, and the ancient sunset
would be engulfed there.
                    His mathematical perplexity
shattered at the horizon
            freed neither the slaves nor the sand.

1978   *(ME)*

'ITEM, MY BODY I DISPOSE AND LEAVE'

    The third Orpheus has hanged himself
with his tennis socks.
                The news lacks decorum
for anyone expecting sobs of stone, bleatings

71

of wild beasts on leashes: the hilarious deathly loop
was traced by nymphs brimming
with fat, hours only after his final set.
'*Item*, my body I dispose and leave,' one reads
under a wisp of lyrical down, the grizzled pubis
further proof of the ravages of age —
                                    and immediately the dogs
are loosed, the net torn, Euridyce spattered
with reddening sands: ravelled, dead.
It might have been a volley, maybe a backhand,
they surmise maliciously.
                        And conversely this is how death
derives from life, from an uninterrupted game,
its sour taste of winter apple.

1978   *(ME)*

DON'T SEND ME MESSAGES

don't send me messages: they're lies;

and these goddam mothers who go and drown themselves,
the light that ruffles among the strawberries,
the wild eyed whirring of the Pope & Co Boston bicycle with
moustaches painted on it and a colonial skull-cap
and a winged Hermes scarf in the wind across the square, and the angel
astride the sundial, or worse still the labyrinth, set
in the lavender paving, and the girl, tall,
straight backed, mouth smeared with greenish water,
murk of that bushy underworld where
ancient katabasis dampnesses dissolve,
insofar as it still remains unproven that the irruption
of the numinous is equivalent to a psychosis, for example:

forget it, the pathos, the password — it's fluttering all
around furry as a cabbage butterfly, can't you see it, it's suffocating us

1978   *(RB, MD)*

PARAGRAPH, ON INDIFFERENCE

happy indifferences, considering the times: the first
and the last, yours, others', hand over fist and
headlong, in the coolness of grass, in the dark flurry
of an autumn morning, likewise those of the cockroach,
of the bat in a paletot, those of the typewriter,
since the notion of sanctity is eccentric, and those
of the dead fig trees slain in the gospel, of moles
who have lost their bearings and the garden,
of sword swallowers, collared natrices,
broodings on the buncumus, together with sleep, in a word
precisely those which are unknowable and, by common agreement,
morbid, so, if you happen to remark in yourself
the ridiculous agony of the prophet, persevere: happy, then,
these leavings-behind, these backs or bookrests of the future,
these graffiti on your no-longer-youth, if they allow you
to weigh up the cons, the limpidity of solitude, the mild
immoral pleasure of not giving way to the obvious shudders,
the uncontrollable deficit — in order that this at least
may remain innocent, the poor sadistic alternative
of being apart, yes, but passionately

1979   *(ME)*

THE USEFULNESS OF THE SNAKE

It is the idea of malignance which gnaws him. Since the beginning,
they have never stopped thinking of that. Attributing to him
unspeakable things, twining them round and round him. He, though,
just goes on thinking: like sparrows, undertakers, little
old ladies, brooms with their barrage of bristles, even
a famous story by Kipling. What is to be done?
When the snaky one goes slithering, in sceptical indolence,
his beady little eye on the inner surface of the definite
or of the indefinite, of the masculine or feminine something,
of the who knows what or whatever, and manages to see the moon,
then does his best to pass through the eye of the needle,

73

even with a soft, suspicious wailing, and around his coils
the crinkled skin cracks open, as he hisses the paradox
of his tongue of the fallen tree — then, in the imperceptible click
made by that split in his sleek, sinuous form, a kind of *craquelé*,
which is itself an ancient model for discourse — it is precisely then,
they say with a pinch of science, bifurcated, political,
that something will, is bound to, is just about to happen... And we
go on hoping it will, go on waiting, do nothing but wait for that
sudden definitive jerk, the new beginning. Nobody, however, celebrates
the rite, bite or poison which, still and evermore, are devoted,
entrusted, so unselfconsciously, to the service of others.
Hence the extreme usefulness of possessing such an animal.

1979   *(RB)*

NOTES

Some of these have been supplied by the author, and some by translators. Ed.

p.15 *The Resolution*. See W.H. Auden's *New Year Letter*, end of part I: 'to all / Who wish to read it anywhere, / And if they open it, En Clair.'

p.17 *Incitatus*. The name of the Emperor Caligula's horse, which he nominated to be a Senator.

p.20 *A Visit to the Ruins of the Roman City of Bath*. The epigraph quotes the anonymous Anglo-Saxon poem 'The Ruin', which is also thought to concern Bath, the Roman *Aquae Sulis*. The fragment is translated in the middle of the poem.

p.22 *Two Figures at the Door*. The epigraph here is by the author, and serves as an extension of the title or *introibo*.

p.23 *The Naviglio Canal at Night*. The Naviglio runs through part of Milan. See also 'A Few Verses for Christmas' below.

p.26 *On the Banks of the Lambro, Thinking of the Funeral Monument of Gaston de Foix*. The Lambro is a stream running through part of Milan. See also 'Thesis' below. Gaston de Foix was a Condottiero (soldier of fortune) whose monument is now in the museum of the Castello Sforcesco in Milan. See also Section XVII of *Information Report*, and the cover design of the English edition (q.v. Bibliography).

p.27 *A Few Verses for Christmas*. Written at Harvard. The Ripa Ticinese is a stretch of bank and road along the Naviglio Canal in Milan.

p.28 *Café Mozart*. 'A little café in Cambridge, Massachusetts, popular with students, writers and musicians, not far from where I was staying. I once met Joan Baez there, when she was quite young, and talked to her.' R.S.

p.31 *Elegy for Vernon Watkins*. Welsh poet, friend of Dylan Thomas, Ceri Richards and Roberto Sanesi. The manner of his death in 1967 (a heart attack while playing tennis during an American visit) is referred to in the poem. Sanesi is Watkins's Italian translator, and many images and themes from Watkins's work are echoed here, particularly from 'Taliesin in Gower', on which Sanesi has written a detailed study. The last line of this English translation echoes 'The Night' by the Welsh Metaphysical poet Henry Vaughan. The translator has benefited from previous English versions by William Alexander and Henry Martin (q.v. Bibliography).

p.33 *From the Notes of Keats Before Writing the 'Ode to a Nightingale'*. As well as Keats's poem, see the note by his friend Charles Brown: 'In the spring of 1819 a nightingale had built her nest near my house. Keats felt a tranquil and continual joy in her song; and one morning he took his chair from the breakfast table to the grass plot under a plum tree, where he sat down for two or three hours. When he came into the house, I perceived he had some scraps of paper in his hand, and these he was quietly thrusting behind the books. On inquiry, I found these scraps, four or five in number, contained his poetic feeling on the song of our nightingale.'

p.35 *Our Lady of King's Road*. Fashionable street full of boutiques in Chelsea, which epitomised the 'swinging sixties' in London, and has now gone seedy. '*Anima uagula blandula*' quotes the first line of a poem by the Roman Emperor Hadrian, addressed to his soul ('Little soul — fleeting away and charming'). This line has become famous through T.S. Eliot's 'Animula', which Sanesi's poem also echoes here, as well as other poems by Eliot.

p.37 *Regulae ad Directionem Ingenii*. 'Règles pour la direction de l'esprit,' or 'Rules for the Direction of the Mind' (Descartes). The poem confronts the (at times excessive) *dolcezza* of the Petrarchan tradition with a certain degree of irony. See also 'Vaucluse' below.

75

p.37 *Ziggurat*. Ur-Nina was a singer and dancer at the Babylonian court who is thought to have been androgynous.

p.38 *Vaucluse*. Fontaine de Vaucluse, in Provence, where Petrarch first met Laura. The 'wretched room / beneath the rock' was the one Petrarch lived in, which is now visited by many tourists. The river referred to is the same one mentioned in Petrarch's famous poem beginning 'Chiare, fresche e dolci acque' ('Clear, fresh and sweet waters').

p.41 *For an Atlas of Descriptive Anatomy*. 'Stereotaxis: the movement of an organism in response to contact with a solid. I read about stereotaxis as an experimental procedure carried out on a Japanese monkey ('Macaca Fuskata') by a certain Professor Kusama, with the aim of obtaining a kind of map of the brain and its reactions. I imagined this as a coloured map of a delicate landscape.' R.S.

p.42 *Thesis*. See note to 'On the Banks of the Lambro' above. The Liffey is the river flowing through Dublin, celebrated by James Joyce.

p.43 *Recitative*. The 'you' in this poem is feminine.

p.46 *Journey Toward the North*. The Lofoten Islands in Norway are near the Arctic Circle.

p.47 *Letter I*. '...the green / leash holding the fish by the tail': see note to 'Historical Courses and Recourses' below.

p.52 *From a Conversation Between Hermes and Menipeus on a Field of Snow*. 'Menipeus of Gadara was a Greek philosopher of the third century B.C. Nothing is left of his writings and all that is known of him has come down to us through admirers and imitators. His conception of life seems to have been deeply pessimistic and his behaviour cynical and mocking.' R.S.

p.53 *The Love-Letter of the Mad Gardener Hans Breittmayer*. A fictional character invented by the author.

p.58 *A Propos of Childhood*. 'Fantomas, the gentleman-thief and hotel-mouse, is a very popular character in French crime and detective fiction. His exploits kept me company in many lonely nights of my childhood, and lit them up with magical images.' R.S.

p.58 *Historical Courses and Recourses*. 'I read somewhere that one day Diogenes presented himself in the *agora* pulling 'a dead herring on a leash'. I don't remember the exact reason given for this behaviour, but can intuit it: through life, each one of us carries 'a dead fish' behind us (the body or the soul, depending on one's point of view). I can't help connecting this story, and the metaphor which derives from it, with an ancient oriental legend in which a king carries a corpse on his shoulders which keeps on setting him problems to solve.' R.S.

p.60 *On the Chance Recovery of a Portrait at Schloss Leopoldskron*. 'A castle at Salzburg, where I first stayed in summer 1958 for a Seminar in American Studies, and have returned since on a number of occasions, including 1975 when the poem was written.' R.S. See also the notes to the English edition of *Information Report*, Section VIII.

p.62 *To Frances Richards, Painter*. English artist who has illustrated poems by the author and the translator. Widow of the Welsh artist Ceri Richards.

p.62 *Letter Fragment, to Osip*. Addressed to Osip Mandelstam, the great Russian poet (1891-1938), who died in or on his way to a Stalinist labour camp. 'Tristia' is the title of one of Mandelstam's collections of poetry, and also a work of Ovid's, written in exile. 'Underwood': a make of typewriter, also referred to by Mandelstam.

p.66 *Beehive: Envoi*. 'Beehive' is also the title of an etching by Graham Sutherland, the English artist to whom the poem is dedicated.

p.68 *Lady Able*: Le Diable. 'The devil has always spoken French.' R.S.

p.68 *The Visit*. 'Written in memory of the great Italian photographer Ugo Mulas, who died of cancer, aged little more than forty. A few days before his death he gave me one of his finest and most moving photographs, and this is described in the poem. The terms from

Greek and from various other ancient or tribal languages (*ecpyrosis*, *ragnarök*, *kalùga*, etc.) all relate to ends, disasters, apocalypse, death, rebirth, etc.' R.S.

p.69 *Towards the Crossing*. 'This sonnet was written after resting by the bank of a small river in Austria. *Selbst* and other references are to the work of C.G. Jung.' R.S.

p.70 *'The Mozart Family', 1780/81*. Title of a painting by J.M. Della Croce, in the Residenz Galerie, Salzburg.

p.71 *Variation on the Theme, 'Weeps on the Desert Ochre and the Salt'*. 'The man who built the pyramids' is a drawing by William Blake. 'Weeps on the desert...' etc. is a line from Dylan Thomas's 'My World is Pyramid'.

p.71 *'Item, My Body I Dispose and Leave'*. The title and the seventh line quote Villon's 'Testament'.

p.73 *The Usefulness of the Snake*. 'The French term 'craquelé' is commonly used to describe the 'cracked skin' on the surface of old oil-paintings.' R.S.

ROBERTO SANESI: A SELECT BIBLIOGRAPHY

This list excludes pamphlets, plaquettes and merely occasional or de luxe editions, but concentrates on the main publications. *Ed.*

A PUBLICATIONS IN ITALIAN

1. POETRY

Il feroce equilibrio, Guanda, Parma, 1957.
Poesie per Athikte, Maestri, Milan, 1959.
Oberon in catene, Schwarz, Milan, 1962.
Otto improvvisi, Maestri, Milan, 1965.
Rapporto informativo, Feltrinelli, Milan, 1966.
L'improvviso di Milano, Guanda, Parma, 1969.
Harrington Gardens Suite, Cerastico, Milan, 1972.
Alterego & altre ipotesi, Munt Press, Samedan/Milan, 1974.
La paura, Cerastico, Milan, 1975.
La cosa scritta, Guanda, Milan, 1977.
Il pied-à-terre di Circe, Il trifoglio, Milan, 1979.
Sull'instabilità del soggetto, Seledizioni, Bologna, 1980.
Recitazione obbligata, Guanda, Milan, 1981.

2. IMAGINATIVE PROSE

La polvere e il giaguaro, Palazzi, Milan, 1972.
Malbianco, Do Soul, Milan, 1980.
Lettera Seconda, Giannotta, Verona, 1980.

3. DRAMA

La rappresentazione per Enrico Quinto, Guanda, Parma, 1967.

4. LITERARY CRITICISM

Dylan Thomas, Lerici, Milan, 1960.
T.S. Eliot, CEI, Milan, 1965.
Byron, CEI, Milan, 1966.
Nella coscia del gigante bianco (a study of Dylan Thomas's poem 'In the White Giant's Thigh'), La Nuova Foglio, Macerata, 1976.
Taliesin a Gower (a study of Vernon Watkins's poem 'Taliesin in Gower') Sandro Maria Rosso, Biella, 1978.

a. Text in Italian only:

Reperti, Edizioni del Triangolo, Milan, 1965.
Diciotto fotografie inedite di Alfons Mucha, Milan, 1979.
Pièce pour Maurice Henry, La Nuova Foglio, Macerata, 1979.
Emilio Scanavino, La Nuova Foglio, Macerata, 1979.
Franco Rognoni, Edizioni Annunciata, Milan, 1980.

b. Text in Italian, with accompanying English translation:

The Graphic Works of Ceri Richards, tr. Richard Burns, Cerastico, Milan, 1973.
Ceri Richards, 1931-1940, tr. Rodney Stringer, La Nuova Foglio, Macerata, 1976.
Sul linguaggio organico di Henry Moore ('On the Organic Language of Henry Moore'), tr. Richard Burns, La Nuova Foglio, Macerata, 1977.
Hans Richter, tr. Rodney Stringer, La Nuova Foglio, Macerata, 1978.
Josè Luis Cuevas, tr. Alan Jones, Zarathustra, Milan, 1978.
Graham Sutherland, tr. Howard Rodger MacLean, Zarathustra, Milan, 1979.

B. TRANSLATIONS INTO ITALIAN FROM ENGLISH

1. POETRY

Dylan Thomas, *Poesie*, Guanda, Parma, 1954.
Dylan Thomas, *Poesie giovanili*, Edizioni del Triangolo, Milan, 1958.
T.S. Eliot, *Poesie*, Bompiani, Milan, 1961.
W.B. Yeats, *Poesie*, Lerici, Milan, 1961.
Walt Whitman, *Poesie scelte*, Nuova Accademia, Milan, 1962.
T.S. Eliot, *Il libro dei gatti tuttofare*, Bompiani, Milan, 1963.
Conrad Aiken, *Il Logos nella Quinta Strada*, Guanda, Parma, 1964.
Hart Crane, *Il ponte*, Guanda, Parma, 1967.
Vernon Watkins, *Poesie*, Guanda, Parma, 1968.
P.B. Shelley, *Adonais e altre poesie*, Rusconi, Milan, 1970.
Archibald MacLeish, *Conquistador*, Guanda, Parma, 1970.
Nathaniel Tarn, *Le belle contraddizioni*, Munt Press, Samedan/Milan, 1974.
Richard Burns, *Avebury*, La Nuova Foglio, Macerata, 1976.
William Blake, *Libri profetici*, Guanda, Milan, 1980.

2. VERSE DRAMAS

W.B. Yeats, *Calvario*, Magenta, Varese, 1960.
Christopher Marlowe, *Tre drammi*, Fabbri, Milan, 1969.

3. ANTHOLOGIES OF POETRY EDITED AND TRANSLATED
BY ROBERTO SANESI
Poeti americani, 1900-1956, Feltrinelli, Milan, 1958.
Poesia inglese del dopoguerra, Schwarz, Milan, 1958.
Poeti inglesi del Novecento, Bompiani, Milan, 1960.
Poeti metafisici inglese del Seicento, Guanda, Parma, 1961.
Poemi anglo-sassoni, Lerici, Milan, 1966.

C. POETRY IN ENGLISH TRANSLATION

(An asterisk after the title denotes mainly longer poems or poem-sequences whose versions are not included in the present selection. Ed.)

Letter from New England*, Origin, No.7, Kyoto, October 1962; tr. Cid Corman.
Elegy for Vernon Watkins*, Guanda, Parma, 1968; tr. Henry Martin.
Eight Improvisations*, Delos, No.3, Austin, Texas, 1968; tr. Cid Corman.
Angels Disturb Me*, Giorgio Upiglio, Milan, 1969; tr. William Alexander.
Hypotheses*, Grosseteste Review, Vol.3, No.3, Lincoln, 1970; tr. Cid Corman.
Information Report*, Cape Goliard, London, 1970; tr. William Alexander.
Journey Toward the North, Gino Cerastico, Milan, 1972; tr. William Alexander.
Elegy for Vernon Watkins*, Antaeus, No.9, New York, Spring 1973, and *New Directions*, No.28, New York, 1974; tr. William Alexander.
Letter to Yewrolinskij and *Following the Tradition of Pantomime*, New Directions, No.28, New York, 1974; tr. William Alexander.
Roberto Sanesi: A Selection, ed. Tim Longville, Grosseteste, Lincoln, 1975, with trs. by William Alexander, Richard Burns, Cid Corman and Vernon Watkins. This includes *Harrington Gardens Suite**, tr. William Alexander.